UNDERSTAND YOUR
Mind AND Body

ADHD

AJ Knight

Explore other books at:
WWW.ENGAGEBOOKS.COM

VANCOUVER, B.C.

WWW.ENGAGEBOOKS.COM

ADHD: Understand Your Mind and Body
Knight, AJ 1995 –
Text © 2023 Engage Books
Design © 2023 Engage Books

Edited by: A.R. Roumanis, Melody Sun and Ashley Lee
Design by: Mandy Christiansen
Consultant: Heather Romero - Child Youth and Family Counsellor

Text set in Montserrat Regular.
Chapter headings set in Hobgoblin.

This book is not meant to replace the advice of a medical professional or be a tool for diagnosis. It is an educational tool to help children understand what they or other people are going through.

FIRST EDITION / FIRST PRINTING

LIBRARY AND ARCHIVES CANADA CATALOGUING IN PUBLICATION

Title: ADHD / AJ Knight.
Names: Knight, AJ, author.
Description: Series statement: Understand your mind and body

Identifiers: Canadiana (print) 20230446973 | Canadiana (ebook) 20230446981
ISBN 978-1-77476-784-9 (hardcover)
ISBN 978-1-77476-785-6 (softcover)
ISBN 978-1-77476-786-3 (epub)
ISBN 978-1-77476-787-0 (pdf)
ISBN 978-1-77878-105-6 (audio)

Subjects:
LCSH: Attention-deficit hyperactivity disorder—Juvenile literature.
LCSH: Attention-deficit-disordered children—Juvenile literature.
LCSH: Attention-deficit hyperactivity disorder—Treatment—Juvenile literature.

Classification: LCC RJ506.H9 K59 2023 | DDC J618.92/8589—DC23

This project has been made possible in part by the Government of Canada.

Canada

Contents

Kids who are not diagnosed often get called "lazy" or a "problem child."

What Is ADHD?

Attention Deficit Hyperactivity Disorder (ADHD) is a disorder that affects people's behavior. It affects everyone differently. ADHD is not an illness or disease. The average age that people are **diagnosed** with ADHD is seven.

KEY WORD

Diagnosed: find out if someone has a medical condition.

There are three main types of ADHD.

1. Inattentive ADHD is when someone has trouble focusing on something that is not interesting to them.

2. Kids with hyperactive-impulsive ADHD often run around or climb on things when they are not supposed to.

3. Combined ADHD is a mix of inattentive ADHD and hyperactive-impulsive ADHD. This is the most common type.

What Causes ADHD?

ADHD tends to run in families. It is one of the most studied childhood conditions, but no one knows what causes it. Some people believe things about its causes that are not true. ADHD is NOT caused by medicines, sugar, allergies, television, or bad parenting.

More people are being diagnosed with ADHD today than in the past. This is because doctors are getting better at spotting the signs. A doctor or **psychologist** can diagnose ADHD by asking questions and doing tests.

KEY WORD

Psychologist: a trained professional who helps people understand and change their behavior.

Boys with ADHD are twice as likely to be diagnosed as girls with ADHD.

How Does ADHD Affect Your Brain?

The **frontal lobe** is a part of the brain that helps with memory, focus, and organization. It also helps with controlling emotions and making decisions. The frontal lobe in people with ADHD may age slower or be smaller than other people's. This means people with ADHD may have a hard time with these tasks.

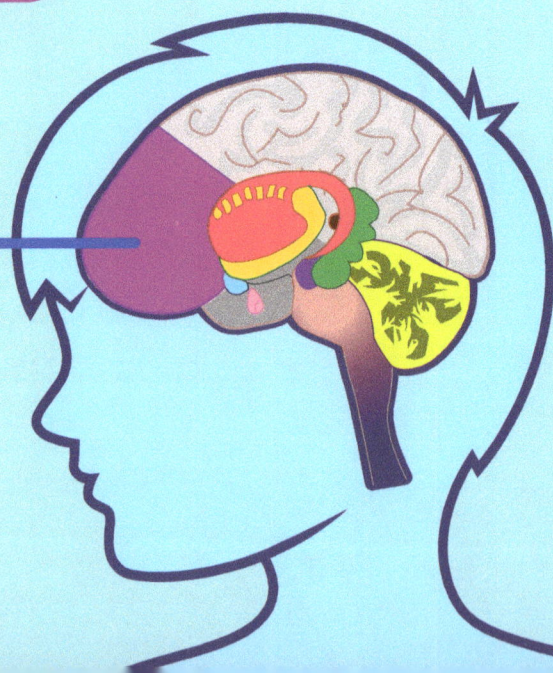

Frontal Lobe

People with ADHD may have less dopamine than others. Dopamine is a brain chemical that helps with a person's mood, memory, attention span, and sleep. Scientists think ADHD brains might use dopamine up faster than non-ADHD brains.

Brain size does not play a role in how smart someone is.

How Does ADHD Affect Your Body?

People with ADHD sometimes have problems with their **motor skills**. They may have messy writing because they have a hard time controlling the pen. They may also have poor balance. This means their bodies have to work harder to stay upright.

KEY WORD

Motor skills: a person's ability to make specific movements with their body.

Poor balance can cause someone to run into objects and hurt themselves.

Many people with ADHD have a lot of energy. They may talk a lot, fidget with their hands, or have a hard time sitting still. This can sometimes make it hard for them to sleep.

Some ADHD medicines may also cause problems with sleeping.

What Does Having ADHD Feel Like?

Someone with ADHD may feel like their thoughts never stop. Their busy minds can sometimes become too much for them to handle. If someone has trouble focusing or is bothered by a noise, they may have a **meltdown**.

KEY WORD

Meltdown: a sudden burst of anger, frustration, or tears.

KEY WORD

Stress: when people feel uncomfortable about something that is happening.

Stimming is when a person makes repeated movements or sounds to help them control their emotions. People with ADHD stim for many reasons. They may do it to help with their focus, to help with **stress**, or because they are happy.

13

Stimulant medicines help with focus and controlling emotions by increasing dopamine in the brain.

Does ADHD Go Away?

Doctors used to think that ADHD only happened in childhood. Now they know that ADHD is for life. Doctors may suggest taking medicines or talking to a **counselor** to help people with ADHD feel more comfortable in the world.

KEY WORD

Counselor: a person who gives advice to others.

ADHD does not go away. But **symptoms** can change as people get older. Adults with ADHD might have less energy. They may still have problems staying organized or paying attention.

KEY WORD

Symptoms: something felt in the body that is a sign of a condition.

Asking for Help

Reaching out can feel scary. But it is important to talk to someone if you are having a hard time. Find a trusted adult to talk to about how you are feeling.

"I keep getting overwhelmed, and I don't know what to do. Can you help?"
"My friend has ADHD, and I think I might have it too. I often forget a thought before I can say it. How can I find out if I have ADHD?"
"I have trouble sitting still and focusing at school. I think I may need more help."

How to Help Others With ADHD

Everyone needs help sometimes. People with ADHD may need different kinds of help than other people. Here are some ways you can help a friend with ADHD.

Be a good listener

Never force someone to talk about their ADHD. If someone chooses to tell you about it, listen to what they have to say.

Encourage them

Celebrate with your friend if they finish a goal they have been working towards. Do not blame them for struggling to complete a task. It is never helpful.

Ask what they need help with

What helps one person with ADHD might not help another. Talk to your friend and learn how you can help them with their specific needs.

The History of ADHD

In 1902, Sir George Frederic Still described a condition in kids that was likely ADHD. Still studied a group of kids that had trouble controlling their behavior. They were impulsive and easily became frustrated or upset.

In 1937, Charles Bradley discovered a stimulant medicine that calmed kids with behavioral differences. He discovered this by mistake while looking for a medicine to help with headaches. Bradley's work led to the discovery of more ADHD medicines about 25 years later.

Ritalin is a stimulant medicine that was discovered in 1944. It was first used for ADHD in the 1950s and 1960s. It is one of the most common stimulant medicines used for ADHD today.

From 1980 to 1978, ADHD was called Attention Deficit Disorder (ADD). The name was changed to ADHD in 1987 to include the word "hyperactivity." The three kinds of ADHD were named in 1994.

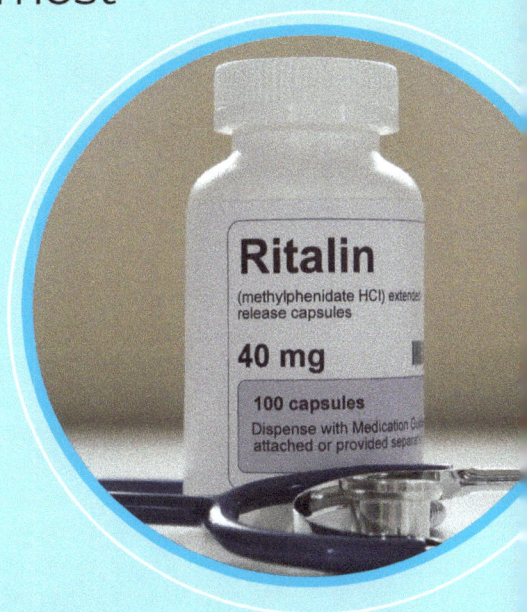

ADHD Superheroes

Not everyone is comfortable talking about their ADHD. Do what feels best for you and respect other people's choices. Here are some ADHD superheroes who openly share their experiences with ADHD.

Bex Taylor-Klaus is an actor with ADHD. They have said that acting is healing for them. Bex hopes kids will accept who they are and not pay attention to what anyone else says.

As of 2023, gymnast **Simone Biles** has won 25 World Championship medals and 7 Olympic medals. She has even been awarded the Presidential Medal of Freedom! Simone has said that no one should feel bad about having ADHD or taking medicine for it.

Adam Levine was diagnosed with ADHD as a teenager. The Maroon 5 lead singer sometimes has trouble paying attention when he is writing and recording. Adam works with a project called "Own It" to help adults who were diagnosed with ADHD as kids.

ADHD Tip 1: Practicing Self-Care

Be patient with yourself. Every day with ADHD will be different. Some days can be easier and some can be harder. Pay attention to how you are feeling, and take breaks when you need to.

Stimming toys can help when you need to focus or calm down. Going for a walk or playing sports can help when you cannot sit still. If remembering to eat is hard, set an alarm to remind you when to have a meal or a snack.

Stimming toys can be a squishy ball, a fidget cube, or even a stuffed animal.

ADHD Tip 2: Making Your Life ADHD-Friendly

Routines are very helpful for people with ADHD. Try making a schedule for yourself each morning. Add fun rewards!

KEY WORD

Routines: doing the same things at the same time each day.

Set a timer when you are doing something boring. That way you know there is an end. Finding yourself a **body double** can also help! It is okay if you have a day where nothing gets done. Each day is different.

KEY WORD

Body double: someone who keeps you company while you work.

ADHD Tip 3: Connecting With Others

Try to find other kids with ADHD at your school or in your neighborhood. You could even attend an online meetup with an adult. This can help you feel less alone.

Building yourself a community can be helpful and fun. There are people with ADHD who understand how you feel. You might even learn something cool about ADHD!

Quiz

Test your knowledge of ADHD by answering the following questions. The questions are based on what you have read in this book. The answers are listed on the bottom of the next page.

1 Is ADHD an illness?

2 Name one type of ADHD.

3 What is a sudden burst of anger, frustration, or tears called?

4 Does ADHD go away?

5 What is one of the most common stimulant medicines used today?

6 What is the name for someone who keeps you company while you work?

Explore Other Level 3 Readers.

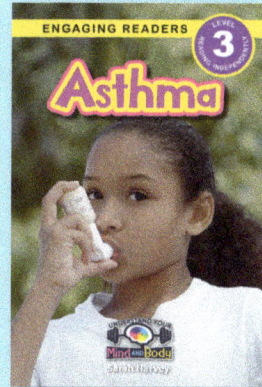

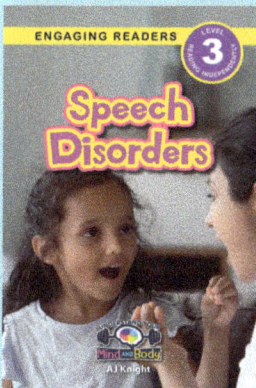

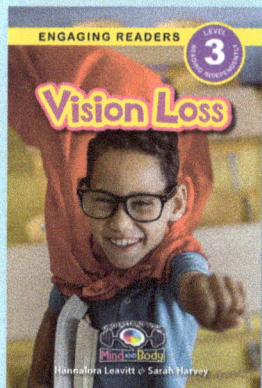

Visit www.engagebooks.com/readers

Answers:
1. No 2. Inattentive, hyperactive-impulsive, or combined 3. A meltdown 4. No 5. Ritalin 6. A body double

www.ingramcontent.com/pod-product-compliance
Lightning Source LLC
Chambersburg PA
CBHW040226040426
42331CB00039B/3362